Mastering Smart Home Integration: Overcoming Compatibility Challenges for a Seamless Experience

Copyright (c) 2024 by James Ordell

All rights reserved. No part of this book may be reproduced in any form or by any electronic or mechanical means, including information storage and retrieval systems, without permission in writing from the publisher, except by a reviewer who may quote brief passages in a review.

3

INTRODUCTION

The Rise of Smart Homes

In recent years, smart home technology has transformed from a futuristic concept into a mainstream reality. What began as simple automation for lights and thermostats has now evolved into a comprehensive ecosystem where nearly every aspect of our homes can be controlled with the tap of a screen or the sound of a voice. From smart locks and security cameras to voice assistants and connected appliances, the possibilities for enhancing comfort, convenience, and security at home are nearly limitless.

For many, the allure of a smart home is the promise of a more efficient, personalized, and secure living environment. Imagine walking into a home where the lights automatically adjust to your preferred brightness, the thermostat sets itself to the perfect temperature, and your favorite playlist starts playing—all without lifting a finger. The idea of having complete control over your home, even when you're miles away, is no longer science fiction but a tangible reality.

Common Frustrations

However, despite the excitement surrounding smart home technology, many users quickly find themselves facing a significant obstacle: compatibility and integration issues. As the market for smart home devices has expanded, so too has the number of brands, platforms, and ecosystems vying for consumers' attention. Unfortunately, not all of these devices are designed to work together seamlessly. A smart thermostat from one brand might not communicate with a security camera from another, leading to a fragmented experience that falls short of the promise of a truly smart home.

These compatibility issues can be a source of frustration for both new and experienced users. Instead of enjoying a cohesive and efficient system, many find themselves juggling multiple apps, struggling with inconsistent performance, or even abandoning certain devices altogether. The lack of standardization across the industry has left many consumers feeling overwhelmed and dissatisfied, unsure of how to make the most of their smart home investments.

Chapter 1: Understanding the Basics of Smart Home Technology

What is a Smart Home?

A smart home refers to a residence equipped with various internet-connected devices that allow homeowners to control and automate functions such as lighting, heating, security, and entertainment systems. These devices communicate with each other through a central network, often managed via a smartphone app or voice assistant, enabling users to monitor and manage their home environment remotely.

At its core, a smart home is designed to make life more convenient, efficient, and secure. Imagine waking up to a home where your coffee starts brewing as soon as your alarm goes off, your thermostat adjusts to the perfect morning temperature, and your lights gradually brighten to ease you into the day. Smart homes are all about bringing automation and personalization into everyday living.

Smart Home Ecosystems

A critical concept in smart home technology is the ecosystem. A smart home ecosystem refers to the interconnected network of devices, apps, and platforms that work together to create a unified smart home experience. The ecosystem is often defined by the central platform or hub that controls and integrates various devices.

Key Ecosystems:

- **Apple HomeKit:** Known for its strong focus on privacy and seamless integration with Apple devices, HomeKit offers a secure ecosystem for users already invested in the Apple ecosystem.

- **Google Home:** Google's ecosystem leverages its powerful AI, providing intuitive voice control through Google Assistant and integration with a wide range of devices.

- **Amazon Alexa:** One of the most widely supported ecosystems, Amazon Alexa offers compatibility with a vast array of devices, making it a versatile choice for building a smart home.

- **Samsung SmartThings:** A flexible platform that works with a broad spectrum of devices, SmartThings is ideal for users looking to integrate products from multiple brands.

Choosing the right ecosystem is crucial because it influences which devices you can use, how they communicate, and the overall ease of integration. While some ecosystems offer broad compatibility, others may be more restrictive but provide tighter security and better performance.

Common Smart Home Devices

The smart home market offers a vast range of devices, each designed to enhance different aspects of home living. Here's a look at some of the most popular categories:

- **Smart Lighting:** Smart bulbs, switches, and dimmers that can be controlled remotely or set to operate on schedules, providing both energy efficiency and convenience.

- **Smart Thermostats:** Devices like the Nest Thermostat or Ecobee allow for precise temperature control, learning your preferences over time to optimize heating and cooling, often leading to energy savings.

- **Smart Security:** Cameras, doorbells, and locks that offer real-time monitoring, alerts, and remote access to ensure your home's safety. Brands like Ring and Arlo are leaders in this space.

- **Smart Speakers and Displays:** Devices like the Amazon Echo, Google Nest Hub, or Apple HomePod that serve as central control points for your smart home, enabling voice commands and providing updates on your connected devices.

- **Smart Appliances:** From refrigerators that can track your groceries to washing machines you can start from your phone, smart appliances add a new level of convenience to daily chores.

- **Smart Plugs and Outlets:** These devices allow you to control regular appliances remotely by turning them on or off via a connected app, making them a simple entry point into smart home technology.

Each of these devices brings its own benefits, and when combined into a cohesive system, they can significantly enhance your home environment. However, the challenge often lies in ensuring these devices work well together, which is where understanding ecosystems and compatibility becomes essential.

Chapter 2: The Compatibility Challenge

Why Compatibility is an Issue

As the smart home industry continues to grow, so does the number of devices and brands competing for market share. While this diversity offers consumers a wide range of choices, it also introduces significant compatibility challenges. Unlike traditional home appliances, which typically operate independently, smart home devices are designed to interact with each other, creating a connected ecosystem. However, not all devices are built to the same standards or with interoperability in mind, leading to frustration for users trying to integrate products from different manufacturers.

One of the primary reasons for compatibility issues is the lack of universal standards in the smart home industry. While there are some common protocols (like Wi-Fi, Zigbee, Z-Wave, and Bluetooth), many devices still rely on proprietary systems that don't easily communicate with other products. This fragmentation forces users to navigate a maze of apps, hubs, and settings, often leading to a less-than-seamless experience.

Additionally, the rapid pace of innovation in the smart home sector means that new devices and features are constantly being introduced. While this is exciting, it also means that older devices may not always be compatible with the latest technology. As a result, users may find that their existing setup becomes outdated or difficult to upgrade without replacing multiple components.

The Impact on Users

For the average consumer, compatibility issues can turn what should be an enjoyable and convenient experience into a source of stress and frustration. Instead of effortlessly controlling their home environment, users might encounter problems such as:

- **Inconsistent Performance:** Devices from different brands may not sync properly, leading to delays, glitches, or outright failures in executing commands. For example, a smart light bulb might not respond to voice commands if it's not fully compatible with the chosen voice assistant.

- **Multiple Apps and Interfaces:** Instead of managing all devices through a single app, users may find themselves juggling multiple apps, each with its own interface and controls. This can be confusing and time-consuming, particularly when troubleshooting issues.

- **Limited Automation and Integration:** One of the key benefits of a smart home is the ability to automate tasks and create integrated routines (e.g., turning off all lights when you leave the house). However, if devices don't communicate effectively, these automations may not work as intended or may be impossible to set up.

- **Security Concerns:** Compatibility issues can also extend to security. If devices are not properly integrated, they may create vulnerabilities in your smart home system, making it easier for unauthorized users to gain access.

- **Increased Costs:** In some cases, users may end up purchasing additional hardware, like smart hubs or bridges, to bridge compatibility gaps. This not only increases the initial investment but can also add complexity to the setup.

Real-Life Scenarios of Compatibility Challenges

To better understand how these issues manifest in real life, let's look at a couple of scenarios:

Scenario 1: The Incompatible Thermostat

- Sarah buys a new smart thermostat to save on energy costs. However, she soon discovers that it doesn't integrate with her existing smart lighting system. As a result, she can't set up an automation where the lights dim when the thermostat detects that she's gone to bed. After spending hours trying to troubleshoot, she ends up using separate apps to control the devices, defeating the purpose of having a unified smart home.

Scenario 2: The Frustrating Upgrade

- John has built his smart home over several years, starting with a few smart plugs and bulbs. When he decides to upgrade to a new smart speaker with better voice recognition, he discovers that the new device isn't fully compatible with some of his older smart plugs. To maintain his setup, he's forced to either replace the older devices or keep the old speaker, which limits his ability to enjoy the latest features.

Scenario 3: The Misbehaving Security System

- Emily invested in a comprehensive smart security system, including cameras, door locks, and motion sensors from different brands, each known for its unique features. However, she quickly discovered that her smart door lock and security camera, which were supposed to work together to provide seamless entry monitoring, weren't compatible. The camera couldn't be triggered by the door lock's activity, meaning she couldn't set up an automation where the camera would start recording whenever the door was unlocked. Additionally, the door lock app was not compatible with her preferred smart home hub, requiring her to use a separate app for this crucial device. Frustrated by the lack of integration, Emily had to manually manage her security system, leading to a less secure and more cumbersome setup.

Scenario 4: The Voice Assistant Dilemma

- Mike is a tech enthusiast who loves using voice assistants to control his smart home. He has invested in a variety of devices, including a smart thermostat, lights, and a media system. Initially, he used Google Assistant to manage everything, but when he received an Amazon Echo as a gift, he decided to switch to Alexa. To his dismay, he discovered that several of his existing devices didn't support Alexa or required complicated workarounds to function. His smart thermostat, for example, didn't integrate with Alexa as seamlessly as it did with Google Assistant, leading to delayed or failed voice commands. Mike found himself having to choose between sticking with Google Assistant or replacing several devices to fully utilize Alexa's capabilities, highlighting the challenge of switching ecosystems once a smart home setup is established.

These scenarios illustrate how compatibility issues can disrupt the smart home experience, leading to frustration and additional costs. However, by understanding the root causes of these problems and taking proactive steps, users can mitigate many of these challenges and create a more harmonious smart home environment.

Chapter 3: Choosing the Right Smart Home Ecosystem

Overview of Major Ecosystems

When building a smart home, one of the most critical decisions you'll make is selecting the ecosystem that will serve as the foundation for your devices and automations. Each ecosystem has its own strengths and weaknesses, and your choice will significantly impact the compatibility, functionality, and ease of use of your smart home. Here's an overview of the major smart home ecosystems:

1. **Apple HomeKit**

  • **Strengths:** HomeKit is known for its strong emphasis on privacy and security, seamlessly integrating with Apple's devices and services. If you're already embedded in the Apple ecosystem (iPhone, iPad, Apple Watch, etc.), HomeKit offers a cohesive and user-friendly experience. The Home app provides a central hub for managing all your devices, and Siri allows for voice control across your smart home.

  • **Weaknesses:** The biggest limitation of HomeKit is its relatively limited compatibility with third-party devices compared to other ecosystems. While the selection is growing, you may find fewer options if you're looking for specific types of devices.

2. **Google Home**

  • **Strengths:** Google Home is powered by Google Assistant, one of the most advanced voice assistants available, known for its ability to understand and execute complex commands. Google Home integrates well with a wide range of third-party devices, and it excels in using AI to create personalized experiences. The Google Home app provides a central place to manage devices, routines, and settings.

- **Weaknesses:** While Google Home supports many devices, some users find that its integration with non-Google products can be inconsistent. Additionally, its privacy policies and data collection practices may be a concern for some users.

3. Amazon Alexa

- **Strengths:** Amazon Alexa boasts the broadest compatibility with third-party smart home devices, making it one of the most versatile ecosystems. With thousands of "skills" (voice commands) available, Alexa can control a wide range of devices and services, from smart lights and thermostats to ordering groceries and playing music. Alexa devices are also generally affordable, making it an accessible option for many users.

- **Weaknesses:** While Alexa's device support is extensive, managing a large number of devices can sometimes be cumbersome. Some users also report that Alexa's voice recognition is not as advanced as Google Assistant's, particularly for complex or nuanced commands.

4. **Samsung SmartThings**

- **Strengths:** SmartThings is a flexible and powerful platform that supports a wide range of devices, including those using Zigbee and Z-Wave protocols. It's ideal for users who want to integrate products from multiple brands into a single, cohesive system. SmartThings' open approach allows for extensive customization, and its app provides a central place to manage devices, routines, and automation.

- **Weaknesses:** The flexibility of SmartThings can be a double-edged sword; its setup and management can be more complex and may require a deeper understanding of smart home technology. Additionally, while it supports many devices, its ecosystem is not as tightly integrated as Apple's or Google's.

Factors to Consider When Choosing an Ecosystem

Selecting the right smart home ecosystem involves weighing various factors based on your specific needs and preferences. Here are some key considerations:

1. **Device Compatibility:**

- Ensure that the ecosystem you choose supports the devices you already own or plan to buy. Check compatibility lists or look for labels that indicate support for your chosen platform (e.g., "Works with Apple HomeKit" or "Works with Google Assistant").

2. **Privacy and Security:**

- Consider how the ecosystem handles your data. Apple HomeKit, for example, is known for its strong privacy protections, while Google and Amazon may collect more data to enhance their services. Choose an ecosystem that aligns with your privacy preferences.

3. **Ease of Use:**

- Some ecosystems are more user-friendly than others. Apple HomeKit, for instance, is designed for simplicity and ease of use, while Samsung SmartThings offers more customization but may require more technical knowledge.

4. **Voice Assistant Preference:**

- If voice control is important to you, consider which voice assistant (Siri, Google Assistant, Alexa) you prefer and which ecosystem integrates best with it. Voice assistants vary in their ability to understand and execute commands, so choose one that meets your needs.

5. **Ecosystem Flexibility:**

- Consider how flexible the ecosystem is in terms of integrating devices from different brands. If you want the freedom to choose from a wide range of products, Amazon Alexa or Samsung SmartThings might be better options than the more closed Apple HomeKit ecosystem.

6. **Future-Proofing:**

- Think about the longevity and future developments of the ecosystem. Some ecosystems, like SmartThings, are more likely to adapt to new standards and technologies, while others might be more restrictive.

Cross-Ecosystem Compatibility

In an ideal world, all smart home devices would work seamlessly together, regardless of brand or platform. While we're not quite there yet, there are ways to build a smart home that operates across multiple ecosystems:

1. **Devices Supporting Multiple Ecosystems:**

- Some devices are designed to be compatible with multiple

ecosystems. For example, smart lights from Philips Hue can be integrated with Apple HomeKit, Google Home, Amazon Alexa, and Samsung SmartThings. Choosing such devices gives you flexibility and future-proofing.

2. Smart Home Hubs:

• Using a smart home hub like Samsung SmartThings can help bridge devices from different ecosystems, allowing you to control them from a single platform. Hubs often support various protocols, making it easier to integrate devices that wouldn't normally work together.

3. Third-Party Apps and Services:

• Apps like IFTTT (If This Then That) or platforms like Home Assistant can help you create custom automations and integrations between devices that are not natively compatible. These tools allow for more complex and personalized smart home setups, although they may require more technical knowledge.

4. Voice Assistant Integration:

• If you prefer using a voice assistant, choose one that supports the widest range of devices. Google Assistant and Amazon Alexa are known for their broad compatibility, allowing you to control devices from different ecosystems with voice commands.

Chapter 4: Smart Home Hubs and Centralized Control

What is a Smart Home Hub?

A Smart Home Hub serves as the central command center of your smart home. It's a device that connects and manages various smart home devices, allowing them to communicate with each other, even if they use different communication protocols like Wi-Fi, Zigbee, or Z-Wave. The hub acts as a bridge between your devices and often provides a single app or interface where you can control and automate your entire smart home system.

The Role of a Smart Home Hub:

- **Centralized Control:** A smart home hub simplifies the management of multiple devices by providing a unified platform. Instead of juggling multiple apps, each corresponding to a different device or brand, you can control everything from one place.

- **Automation:** Hubs enable the creation of complex automation routines that involve multiple devices. For example, you can set a routine where your smart lights dim, your smart lock secures the doors, and your thermostat adjusts the temperature—all with a single command.

- **Enhanced Compatibility:** By supporting multiple communication protocols, a hub can integrate devices from various manufacturers into one cohesive system. This compatibility is crucial for creating a seamless smart home experience.

- **Improved Security:** Some hubs offer additional security features, such as encrypted communication between devices, which can provide peace of mind in a world where cybersecurity concerns are paramount.

Top Smart Home Hubs

When choosing a smart home hub, it's important to consider its compatibility, ease of use, and the extent of automation capabilities. Here's a look at some of the top smart home hubs available today:

1. **Samsung SmartThings**

- **Overview:** Samsung SmartThings is one of the most popular smart home hubs on the market, known for its versatility and wide compatibility. It supports a broad range of devices, including those using Zigbee, Z-Wave, and Wi-Fi protocols.

- **Strengths:** SmartThings excels in flexibility and scalability. It allows you to integrate hundreds of devices from various brands into a single system. The SmartThings app is user-friendly and offers powerful automation capabilities, enabling you to create detailed routines and scenarios.

- **Weaknesses:** The flexibility of SmartThings can make it a bit complex for beginners. Additionally, while it's highly customizable, some users may find the setup process daunting, especially if they are trying to integrate a large number of devices.

- **Ideal For:** Users looking for a powerful, flexible hub that supports a wide range of devices and offers extensive customization options.

2. **Hubitat Elevation**

- **Overview:** Hubitat Elevation is a hub designed for users who prioritize privacy, local control, and advanced automation capabilities. Unlike many hubs that rely on cloud services, Hubitat processes automations locally, meaning your devices can function even if your internet connection goes down.

- **Strengths:** The local processing of Hubitat offers faster response times and greater privacy, as your data isn't sent to the cloud. It supports both Zigbee and Z-Wave devices and provides advanced automation features through its intuitive Rule Machine.

- **Weaknesses:** Hubitat's focus on local control and advanced features can make it less user-friendly for beginners. The interface is not as polished as some other hubs, and there may be a steeper learning curve.

- **Ideal For:** Tech-savvy users who value privacy, local control, and the ability to create complex automations.

3. **Wink Hub 2**

- **Overview:** Wink Hub 2 is designed to be a user-friendly hub that supports a variety of protocols, including Wi-Fi, Bluetooth, Zigbee, Z-Wave, and Lutron Clear Connect. It aims to offer a simple, intuitive interface for controlling smart home devices.

- **Strengths:** Wink Hub 2 is known for its easy setup and user-friendly app, making it a good choice for those new to smart home technology. It supports a wide range of devices, making it a versatile option for building a smart home.

- **Weaknesses:** Wink's cloud-based operation means that your smart home setup is dependent on Wink's servers being operational. Additionally, the company has experienced some financial instability in recent years, leading to concerns about long-term support.

- **Ideal For:** Beginners who want a straightforward, easy-to-use hub with broad device compatibility.

Setting Up a Smart Home Hub

Setting up a smart home hub can seem intimidating, but with the right approach, it can be a straightforward process. Here's a step-by-step guide to help you get started:

Step 1: Choose the Right Hub

- **Consider Compatibility:** Before purchasing a hub, ensure that it is compatible with the devices you currently own or plan to buy. Check whether the hub supports the necessary protocols (e.g., Zigbee, Z-Wave, Wi-Fi).

- **Evaluate Features:** Think about what you want from your smart home system. Do you need advanced automation? Are you concerned about privacy? Choose a hub that aligns with your priorities.

Step 2: Set Up the Hub

- **Unbox and Power On:** Start by unboxing your hub and plugging it into a power source. Many hubs also need to be connected to your home's Wi-Fi router via an Ethernet cable.

- **Download the App:** Most hubs come with a companion app that you'll need to download onto your smartphone or tablet. This app will guide you through the setup process.

- **Create an Account:** If required, create an account with the hub's service provider. This will allow you to manage your devices remotely and set up automations.

Step 3: Connect Devices to the Hub

- **Pairing Devices:** Begin by adding devices to your hub. This process varies depending on the device and hub, but generally involves putting the device into pairing mode (e.g., pressing a button on the device) and then using the hub's app to discover and add the device.

- **Assigning Rooms or Zones:** Many hubs allow you to organize devices by room or zone, which can make managing and automating them easier. For example, you might group all your living room devices together.

- **Naming Devices:** Give each device a clear, descriptive name. This will help you easily identify and control them within the app and when using voice commands.

Step 4: Create Automations

- **Simple Automations:** Start by setting up basic automations, such as turning on the lights when you arrive home or adjusting the thermostat at night. Use the app's automation or routine features to create these scenarios.

- **Advanced Automations:** Once you're comfortable, explore more complex automations involving multiple devices. For example, you could create a "Movie Night" routine that dims the lights, lowers the blinds, and turns on the TV with a single command.

- **Testing:** After setting up your automations, test them to ensure they work as expected. Make any necessary adjustments to timing, triggers, or device settings.

Step 5: Troubleshooting

- **Connectivity Issues:** If a device doesn't connect properly, try resetting it and moving it closer to the hub during setup. Ensure your hub and devices have the latest firmware updates.

- **Performance Tweaks:** If you experience lag or unresponsiveness, consider reducing the number of devices on your network or upgrading your Wi-Fi setup. Some hubs also allow you to prioritize certain devices for better performance.

Step 6: Maintain and Expand

- **Regular Updates:** Keep your hub and devices updated with the latest firmware to ensure they operate smoothly and securely.

- **Expand Gradually:** As you become more familiar with your hub, gradually add more devices to your smart home system. Consider adding sensors, cameras, or additional automation routines to enhance your setup.

By understanding the role of smart home hubs, reviewing top options, and following a structured setup process, you can build a smart home that is not only functional but also efficient and user-friendly. With the right hub, managing your smart home becomes a seamless experience, allowing you to enjoy the full benefits of smart technology.

Chapter 5: Integration Strategies for Multi-Brand Devices

As smart home technology continues to evolve, it's increasingly common for users to have devices from different brands and ecosystems in their homes. While each brand may offer its own unique strengths, integrating these diverse devices into a unified system can be challenging. This chapter provides strategies to create a seamless smart home experience, step-by-step integration guides, and tips on using automation tools like IFTTT to bridge compatibility gaps.

Creating a Unified Experience

To create a cohesive smart home system with multi-brand devices, it's essential to focus on three key strategies: compatibility, centralization, and automation.

1. **Compatibility:**

- **Research Before Purchase:** Before adding a new device to your smart home, check its compatibility with your existing system. Look for devices that support common communication protocols like Zigbee, Z-Wave, or Wi-Fi, as these are more likely to integrate smoothly.

- **Use Compatible Hubs:** Consider investing in a smart home hub that supports multiple protocols and brands. Hubs like Samsung SmartThings or Hubitat Elevation are designed to integrate devices from different manufacturers, helping you avoid potential compatibility issues.

- **Cross-Platform Support:** Some devices and apps are designed to work across multiple platforms. For example, certain smart lights or thermostats may be compatible with Google Home, Amazon Alexa, and Apple HomeKit, allowing you to control them regardless of the ecosystem you prefer.

2. **Centralization:**

- **Unified Control Interface:** Centralize control by using a hub or a single app that can manage all your devices. This eliminates the need to switch between different apps for different brands, streamlining the user experience.

- **Voice Assistants:** Utilize voice assistants like Amazon Alexa, Google Assistant, or Apple Siri to control devices from different brands.

Voice commands can be a powerful tool for integrating multi-brand devices into a unified system, as they allow you to control various devices simultaneously.

- **Scenes and Routines:** Create scenes or routines that involve devices from different brands. For instance, you can set up a "Goodnight" routine that locks your smart door, turns off the lights, and adjusts the thermostat, even if these devices are from different manufacturers.

3. **Automation:**

- **Smart Hub Automations:** Use your smart hub's automation features to create custom routines that involve devices from different ecosystems. For example, a motion sensor from one brand can trigger smart lights from another brand to turn on when you enter a room.

- **Third-Party Tools:** Leverage third-party automation platforms like IFTTT (If This Then That) to bridge gaps between devices that might not natively integrate with each other. These tools can help you create automations that bring together disparate devices into a single workflow.

Step-by-Step Integration Guides

Integrating devices across different ecosystems requires careful planning and execution. Below are step-by-step guides to help you connect and sync multi-brand devices.

Guide 1: Integrating Smart Lights with Different Hubs

1. **Identify Your Devices:**

- List the smart lights you have and their respective brands. Determine which hub (if any) supports these lights. For example, you might have Philips Hue bulbs and LIFX bulbs, which typically operate on different hubs or apps.

2. **Connect to the Hub:**

- **Philips Hue:** Use the Philips Hue Bridge to connect your Hue bulbs. Plug the bridge into your router, download the Philips Hue app, and follow the on-screen instructions to add your bulbs.

- **LIFX Bulbs:** LIFX bulbs are Wi-Fi enabled and do not require a hub. Simply download the LIFX app, connect your bulbs to your Wi-Fi network, and follow the setup process in the app.

3. **Create Scenes Across Platforms:**

- Use a hub like SmartThings or a voice assistant like Amazon Alexa that supports both Philips Hue and LIFX. Create a "Movie Night" scene where the Hue bulbs dim to 30% and the LIFX bulbs change color to a soft blue, all triggered by a single command.

4. **Test and Adjust:**

- Once your scene is set up, test it to ensure that all lights respond as expected. Make adjustments in the app or hub as necessary.

Guide 2: Synchronizing a Smart Thermostat and Smart Lock

1. **Install and Set Up Devices:**

- **Smart Thermostat:** Install your smart thermostat (e.g., Nest or Ecobee) and connect it to your home Wi-Fi network using the manufacturer's app. Complete the setup process by entering your preferences and scheduling your desired temperatures.

- **Smart Lock:** Install your smart lock (e.g., August or Schlage) and connect it to your Wi-Fi or Bluetooth using the manufacturer's app. Set up user codes and preferences in the app.

2. **Integrate with a Smart Hub:**

- If both devices are compatible with a smart hub like SmartThings, add them to the hub. Follow the hub's instructions to ensure both the thermostat and lock are connected and recognized.

3. **Create an Automation:**

- Set up an automation where locking the smart lock triggers the thermostat to switch to "Away" mode, adjusting the temperature to conserve energy while you're out. This can usually be done within the hub's app or through a third-party service like IFTTT.

4. **Test the Automation:**

- Test the automation by locking the door and checking if the thermostat adjusts the temperature accordingly. Make any necessary tweaks to the timing or conditions in the automation settings.

Guide 3: Connecting Multi-Brand Cameras and Sensors

1. **Setup Individual Devices:**

- **Cameras:** Install your smart cameras (e.g., Arlo, Ring) following the manufacturer's guidelines. Connect them to your Wi-Fi network and configure them through the respective apps.

- **Sensors:** Install sensors (e.g., motion sensors from Ecolink or door/window sensors from Aeotec) and connect them to your hub or directly to your network.

2. **Use a Hub or Platform for Integration:**

- If using a hub that supports all your devices, add both cameras and sensors to the hub. Alternatively, use a platform like IFTTT to link these devices if they don't natively support integration.

3. **Set Up Triggers and Notifications:**

- Create automations where motion detected by the sensor triggers the camera to start recording. You can also set up notifications to alert you when this automation is activated.

4. **Fine-Tune Settings:**

- Adjust the sensitivity of the sensors and the recording duration of the cameras to suit your needs. Test the setup by simulating motion or opening a door/window to ensure the integration works smoothly.

Using IFTTT and Other Automation Tools

IFTTT (If This Then That) is a powerful, user-friendly platform that allows you to create automations, known as "applets," between devices and services that might not otherwise be compatible. Here's how to leverage IFTTT and similar tools to enhance your smart home integration.

Understanding IFTTT:

- **How It Works:** IFTTT operates on a simple premise—if one event happens (the trigger), it causes another event to occur (the action). For example, "If motion is detected by your Ring camera, then turn on your Philips Hue lights."

- **Wide Range of Services:** IFTTT connects with thousands of devices and services, including smart home products, social media platforms, weather services, and more. This makes it a versatile tool for bridging compatibility gaps.

Creating an IFTTT Applet:

1. **Sign Up and Log In:**

- Create an account on the IFTTT website or app, and log in to access the platform's features.

2. **Select a Trigger:**

- Choose the device or service that will trigger the automation. For example, select your smart camera detecting motion as the trigger.

3. **Select an Action:**

- Choose the device or service that will perform the action. For example, you might select your smart lights turning on as the action.

4. **Customize and Save:**

- Customize the applet by adjusting settings such as trigger sensitivity or action duration. Once satisfied, save the applet, and it will begin running immediately.

Advanced Automation Tools:

- **Home Assistant:** For users who want more control and customization, Home Assistant is an open-source platform that allows for highly detailed automations and integrations. It supports a wide range of devices and can be customized extensively through scripting.

- **Stringify:** Although no longer active, Stringify was a platform similar to IFTTT that allowed for more complex workflows by linking multiple triggers and actions. Current alternatives or advancements in platforms like Home Assistant or Node-RED may offer similar capabilities.

Expanding Your Automations:

- **Combine Multiple Applets:** You can create a series of applets to build more complex automations. For instance, you could set up one applet to turn on lights when motion is detected and another to send you a notification simultaneously.

- **Explore IFTTT Pro:** For more advanced users, IFTTT Pro offers features like multi-step applets, conditional logic, and faster execution, allowing for even more sophisticated smart home integrations.

Using IFTTT and other automation tools, you can enhance the functionality of your smart home system, ensuring that devices from different brands work together harmoniously. This not only maximizes the utility of your devices but also creates a more seamless and enjoyable smart home experience.

Chapter 6: Troubleshooting Common Integration Issues

As you build and expand your smart home system, it's inevitable that you'll encounter integration issues. These problems can arise from various sources, including device compatibility, outdated firmware, or network-related challenges. This chapter will guide you through diagnosing common integration issues, the importance of firmware and software updates, and addressing network-related problems to ensure your smart home operates smoothly.

Identifying Problems

When something goes wrong in your smart home setup, the first step is to accurately diagnose the issue. This can involve a process of elimination, checking connections, and ensuring that all devices are properly configured.

1. **Common Symptoms of Integration Issues:**

- **Unresponsive Devices:** A device fails to respond to commands from your hub or app, or it does not trigger automation routines as expected.

- **Connectivity Loss:** Devices frequently disconnect from the network or lose their connection to the smart home hub.

- **Automation Failures:** Automations or routines don't execute as planned, such as lights not turning on at the scheduled time or doors not locking automatically.

- **Lagging Performance:** There is a noticeable delay between issuing a command and the device responding, indicating potential communication issues.

2. **Steps to Diagnose the Issue:**

- **Check Device Status:** Start by checking the status of the unresponsive or malfunctioning device in the hub's app. Ensure the device is powered on and connected to the network. Some hubs provide diagnostic tools that can help you pinpoint the problem.

- **Test Manual Operation:** If possible, try to operate the device manually. For example, if a smart light isn't responding to an app command, see if it works using a physical switch. This can help determine whether the issue is with the device itself or its communication with the network.

- **Review Automation Logs:** Many smart home hubs and apps offer logs or history features that track automation events. Reviewing these logs can help you identify when and where an automation failed, providing clues to the root cause.

- **Isolate the Device:** Temporarily remove the problematic device from your smart home system and test the system's functionality without it. If the issue persists, the problem may lie elsewhere in your network or setup.

3. **Common Causes of Integration Issues:**

- **Compatibility Conflicts:** Devices from different brands or ecosystems might not integrate smoothly, especially if they rely on different communication protocols.

- **Interference:** Wireless signals can be disrupted by physical obstacles, other electronic devices, or even network congestion, leading to communication problems.

- **Outdated Firmware/Software:** Devices running on outdated firmware or apps with bugs can cause inconsistencies in performance.

Firmware and Software Updates

Keeping your smart home devices and apps updated is crucial for maintaining their functionality, security, and compatibility. Here's why updates matter and how to perform them.

1. **Why Firmware and Software Updates Are Important:**

• **Bug Fixes:** Manufacturers frequently release updates to fix bugs that can cause devices to malfunction or lose connection.

• **Security Patches:** Updates often include security patches that protect your devices from vulnerabilities that could be exploited by hackers.

• **Improved Compatibility:** As smart home technology evolves, updates ensure that your devices remain compatible with new hubs, platforms, and other devices in your ecosystem.

• **New Features:** Updates can also introduce new features or enhance existing ones, allowing you to get more out of your devices.

2. **How to Perform Updates:**

• **Automatic Updates**: Many smart home devices and apps are set to update automatically by default. Ensure that automatic updates are enabled in the device settings or the app to keep your devices current.

- **Manual Updates:** For devices that require manual updates, follow these general steps:

- **Check for Updates:** Open the device's companion app and navigate to the settings or device info section. Look for an option to check for firmware or software updates.

- **Download and Install:** If an update is available, download and install it directly from the app. Ensure the device remains powered on and connected to the network throughout the process.

- **Restart the Device:** After the update is complete, it may be necessary to restart the device to apply the changes.

- **Hub Updates:** Don't forget to update your smart home hub's firmware as well. Hubs are central to device communication, so keeping them updated is essential for overall system stability.

3. **Common Update Issues and Solutions:**

- **Failed Updates:** If an update fails, check your network connection and try again. Ensure the device has enough battery or power and isn't interrupted during the update process.

- **Post-Update Problems:** If a device malfunctions after an update, try restarting the device or performing a factory reset. In some cases, rolling back to a previous firmware version may resolve the issue, although this is generally not recommended unless absolutely necessary.

- **Delayed Updates:** Some updates are rolled out gradually by manufacturers. If you haven't received an update yet, check the manufacturer's website or community forums for information on when it will be available to your region or device model.

Network Considerations

A strong, reliable network is the backbone of any smart home system. Network-related issues can lead to communication breakdowns between devices, causing them to become unresponsive or slow. Here's how to address these challenges.

1. **Understanding Network Requirements:**

- **Bandwidth:** Smart home devices, particularly those that stream video (e.g., cameras), require sufficient bandwidth to function properly. Ensure your internet plan can handle the load, especially if multiple devices are in use simultaneously.

- **Wi-Fi Coverage:** The placement of your router and the strength of your Wi-Fi signal are critical. Devices that are too far from the router or in areas with poor signal strength may have trouble staying connected.

2. **Improving Network Performance:**

- **Optimize Router Placement:** Place your Wi-Fi router in a central location within your home to ensure even coverage. Avoid placing it near large metal objects or appliances that can interfere with the signal.

- **Use Mesh Networks:** If your home has multiple floors or dead spots, consider upgrading to a mesh network system. Mesh networks use multiple nodes placed around your home to provide consistent Wi-Fi coverage in all areas.

- **Segment Your Network:** Create separate Wi-Fi networks for your smart home devices and personal devices. This can reduce network congestion and prevent bandwidth-hogging devices from affecting the performance of your smart home system.

3. **Troubleshooting Network Issues:**

- **Check Device Connectivity:** Use your smart home app or hub to check the connection status of each device. If a device is frequently losing connection, try moving it closer to the router or adding a Wi-Fi extender.

- **Reboot Your Network:** Power cycle your router and modem by unplugging them for 30 seconds and then plugging them back in. This can resolve temporary network issues.

- **Change Wi-Fi Channels:** Interference from neighboring Wi-Fi networks can cause connectivity problems. Access your router settings and switch to a less congested Wi-Fi channel to improve signal clarity.

- **Upgrade Your Router:** If your router is old or doesn't support the latest Wi-Fi standards, consider upgrading to a newer model. A modern router will provide better performance and support for more devices.

4. **Dealing with Interference:**

- **Identify Sources of Interference:** Common sources of wireless interference include microwaves, cordless phones, baby monitors, and even thick walls. Identify and reduce or eliminate these sources where possible.

- **Switch to Wired Connections:** For devices that require a stable connection (e.g., smart hubs, streaming devices), consider using Ethernet instead of Wi-Fi. Wired connections are more reliable and less prone to interference.

- **Zigbee and Z-Wave Networks:** If using Zigbee or Z-Wave devices, ensure they are operating on channels that don't overlap with your Wi-Fi network. Most hubs allow you to change the Zigbee/Z-Wave channel in the settings to reduce interference.

You can minimize disruptions and maintain a smoothly functioning smart home by understanding how to diagnose integration issues, keeping your devices updated, and optimizing your network. Troubleshooting these common problems effectively ensures that your devices work together seamlessly, providing the convenience and automation you expect from your smart home system.

Chapter 7: Future-Proofing Your Smart Home

In the rapidly evolving world of smart home technology, staying ahead of the curve is essential to ensure that your investment continues to serve you well into the future. As new standards emerge, devices evolve, and your needs change, future-proofing your smart home will help you avoid compatibility issues, ensure device longevity, and make room for seamless expansion. This chapter covers strategies for preparing for new standards, selecting devices with staying power, and planning for future additions to your smart home ecosystem.

Preparing for New Standards

One of the biggest challenges in smart home technology has been the lack of a unified standard, leading to compatibility issues between devices from different manufacturers. However, this landscape is beginning to change with the introduction of new standards designed to simplify and unify smart home ecosystems.

1. **Understanding Emerging Standards:**

- **Matter:** Matter is a new open-source, royalty-free connectivity standard developed by the Connectivity Standards Alliance (CSA), previously known as the Zigbee Alliance. It aims to create a universal language for smart home devices, allowing them to communicate with each other regardless of brand or platform. Matter promises to reduce compatibility issues and make it easier to integrate new devices into your existing setup.

- **Thread:** Thread is another emerging standard designed to improve smart home connectivity. Unlike traditional Wi-Fi or Bluetooth, Thread creates a low-power, mesh network that enhances reliability and reduces latency. It works in tandem with Matter to provide a more robust and resilient smart home network.

2. **Benefits of Adopting New Standards:**

- **Increased Interoperability:** By adopting devices that support Matter and Thread, you can reduce the risk of compatibility issues as these standards become widely adopted across the industry.

- **Simplified Setup:** Devices adhering to these new standards will be easier to set up and integrate, reducing the complexity of managing a multi-brand smart home system.

- **Future Compatibility:** As more manufacturers embrace these standards, future devices are more likely to work seamlessly with your existing setup, reducing the need for frequent upgrades or replacements.

3. **Preparing for the Transition:**

- **Identify Matter-Compatible Devices:** As Matter and Thread gain traction, start looking for devices that are certified to support these standards. Many major brands are beginning to roll out updates or new products that are Matter-compatible.

- **Update Existing Devices:** Some existing devices may receive firmware updates to support Matter. Check with the manufacturers of your current devices to see if updates are available or planned.

- **Stay Informed:** Keep an eye on developments in smart home technology. As Matter and Thread become more widespread, additional resources and tools will become available to help you transition your smart home system.

Choosing Devices with Longevity

When building or expanding your smart home, it's important to select devices that are likely to remain compatible with future technologies and standards. Here's how to choose wisely to maximize the lifespan of your investments.

1. **Look for Industry Support:**

- **Major Ecosystem Backing:** Choose devices that are part of major smart home ecosystems like Amazon Alexa, Google Home, or Apple HomeKit. These platforms are more likely to continue receiving support and updates as technology evolves.

- **Future-Proof Standards:** As mentioned earlier, opt for devices that support emerging standards like Matter and Thread. These standards are designed with longevity in mind, making them safer bets for the future.

2. **Evaluate Manufacturer Commitment:**

- **Reputation for Updates:** Research manufacturers' track records for providing firmware updates and ongoing support for their products. Brands that consistently update their devices are more likely to ensure compatibility with future technologies.

- **Long-Term Vision:** Some manufacturers are known for their commitment to future-proofing their products. Look for companies that clearly communicate their plans for supporting new standards or expanding their product ecosystems.

3. **Modularity and Upgradability:**

- **Modular Design:** Devices with a modular design allow for easier upgrades. For example, some smart home hubs or routers offer interchangeable components that can be upgraded as technology advances.

- **Backward Compatibility:** Consider devices that are backward-compatible with older standards or protocols. This ensures that even as new technologies emerge, your existing devices can still function within your system.

4. **Avoid Proprietary Systems:**

- **Proprietary Risks:** Be cautious of devices that rely heavily on proprietary systems or protocols, as they may become obsolete if the manufacturer discontinues support. Instead, favor products that adhere to widely adopted standards and protocols.

5. **Sustainability and Longevity:**

- **Durable Construction:** Choose devices built with high-quality materials that are likely to withstand the test of time. Well-constructed devices not only last longer but also reduce the environmental impact of frequent replacements.

- **Manufacturer Support:** Some manufacturers offer repair services, spare parts, or extended warranties, indicating a commitment to the longevity of their products. Investing in such devices can save you money and hassle in the long run.

Planning for Expansion

As your smart home needs grow, it's important to plan for the addition of new devices and capabilities without disrupting your current setup. Here's how to prepare for future expansion while maintaining system stability and performance.

1. **Assess Your Current System:**

- **Evaluate Capacity:** Before adding new devices, assess your current system's capacity. Ensure that your smart home hub, network, and power supply can handle additional devices without causing performance issues.

- **Identify Gaps:** Consider areas of your home that could benefit from smart devices you don't currently have. For example, if you've already automated lighting and security, you might look into smart appliances, window treatments, or energy management systems.

2. **Scalability Considerations:**

- **Choose Scalable Hubs:** If you plan to expand your smart home, invest in a hub that supports a large number of devices and offers strong network capabilities. Hubs like SmartThings and Hubitat are designed with scalability in mind, making them ideal for growing systems.

- **Network Expansion:** Consider upgrading to a mesh Wi-Fi system if you haven't already. As you add more devices, especially in larger homes, a mesh network will ensure consistent connectivity across all areas.

3. **Organize and Label Devices:**

- **Stay Organized:** As your system grows, keeping track of devices can become challenging. Use clear and consistent naming conventions in your smart home apps and hubs to easily identify and manage each device.

- **Documentation:** Maintain a list or spreadsheet of all your smart devices, including their locations, manufacturers, and firmware versions. This will help you manage updates and troubleshoot issues more effectively.

4. **Test New Devices Before Full Integration:**

- **Pilot Testing:** When adding a new device, test it in isolation before fully integrating it into your smart home system. This allows you to identify potential compatibility issues without affecting your entire setup.

- **Gradual Integration:** Add new devices gradually rather than all at once. This approach makes it easier to troubleshoot any issues that arise and ensures that each device integrates smoothly into your existing ecosystem.

5. **Automation and Routines:**

- **Expand Existing Automations:** As you add new devices, consider how they can be integrated into your existing automation routines. For example, if you add smart blinds, you can include them in your "Good Morning" routine alongside your lights and thermostat.

- **Create New Scenarios:** Think about new automation scenarios that weren't possible before. For instance, adding smart water sensors and shutoff valves could enable a "Leak Detection" automation that prevents water damage.

6. **Stay Flexible:**

- **Adapt to Change:** The smart home landscape is constantly evolving, so it's important to stay flexible and open to change. Be prepared to adopt new technologies, standards, and devices as they emerge.

- **Consider Professional Consultation:** If you're planning a significant expansion or renovation of your smart home, consider consulting with a professional smart home installer. They can help you design a system that's both robust and future-proof.

By preparing for new standards, choosing devices with longevity in mind, and planning for future expansion, you can ensure that your smart home remains adaptable and functional for years to come. Future-proofing your smart home not only protects your investment but also allows you to take full advantage of the latest technological advancements as they become available.

www.ingramcontent.com/pod-product-compliance
Lightning Source LLC
Chambersburg PA
CBHW070416230526
45471CB00006B/2833